Go To Joseph

10 Day Preparation for Consecration to St. Joseph

Go To Joseph

10 Day Preparation for Consecration to St. Joseph

Renzo Ortega

TwoBecomeFamily.com
@twobecomefamily

Go To Joseph: 10 Day Preparation for Consecration to St. Joseph by Renzo Ortega

The publisher has applied for a *nihil ostat* and *imprimatur*. When they are granted, the details will be noted here.

Copyright © 2021 Two Become Family, LLC. All rights reserved.

Except for quotations, no part of this work may be reproduced, transmitted, or stored in any form whatsoever without the prior written permission from the publisher.

All other Scripture quotations are taken from the Revised Standard Version: Second Catholic Edition (RSV-CE) of the Bible, copyright ©2006 by the Division of Christian Education of the National Council of Churches of Christ in the United States of America. All rights reserved.

If any copyrighted materials have been inadvertently used in this work without proper credit being given in one manner or another, please notify the publisher in writing so that future printings of this work may be corrected accordingly.

Copyright © 1961;1989; 2005; 2020 Libreria Editrice Vaticana, 00120 Citta del Vaticano, for the original texts of John XXIII, John Paul II, and His Holiness Pope Francis the texts may be found on the Vatican website: www.vatican.va

Cover design by Jaimee Keogler – thesimplesaints.com
Edited by Katie Keogler and Monica Ortega

ISBN: 978-0-578-88237-6
Published in the United States by
Two Become Family, LLC

www.TwoBecomeFamily.com

Printed in the United States of America

For my wife, Monica, and our children, Kolbe, John Paul, Gianna, Thomas and Benedict.

Thank you for making me better, you all are the best part of my day.

"Go to Joseph; what he says to you, do."
-Genesis 41:55

Contents

Why I Wrote a Book About St. Joseph		1
Introduction to Consecration to St. Joseph		8
Day 1	Matthew 1:1,16	17
Day 2	Luke 1:26-27	25
Day 3	Luke 1:34-35	30
Day 4	Matthew 1:20	36
Day 5	Matthew 2:13-14	43
Day 6	Luke 1:34	49
Day 7	Matthew 1:25	57
Day 8	Luke 2:48-49	63
Day 9	Luke 2:50-52	70
Day 10	Matthew 13:55	76
Consecration Day		82
Act of Consecration		85
Prayers to St. Joseph		90
About the Author		99
About Two Become Family		101

Why I Wrote a Book About St. Joseph

I was born and raised Catholic. I went to Catholic school, was an altar server, and was involved in my parish's youth group. Despite my Catholic upbringing, I didn't know Jesus. I knew a lot about Jesus, but He was more like a character in a book, than my Savior.

In high school, my lack of faith led me to question a lot of things. I was uncertain about who I was, and where I was going. This led me to question whether I had what it took to enter adulthood. As a young man, I questioned whether or not I had what it took to be man.

Going into my senior year, I become more and more aware of the baggage I was carrying. Thanks be to God I went to a Steubenville Conference that Summer. That led me to Jesus, to my beautiful bride, and to an entirely different trajectory of life. Jesus was finally real to me.

But my conversion didn't end with my encounter with Jesus. Usually the first time we meet Christ is a beginning, not an end. God wasn't done with me.

Not So Happily-Ever-After

Ten years later, in 2016, I was devoted to my Catholic faith, and married to my best friend, but utterly failing in my vocation. As a couple, Monica and I wasted a lot of the time we spent together while dating and engaged. We didn't take time to cultivate the boundaries, habits, and virtues necessary for a healthy marriage before we said our vows. We kind of thought marriage was just a bigger and better engagement and that Jesus would make it work if we couldn't. It was supposed to be easy. That mindset left us struggling to share space once we were past the honeymoon period. Despite our faith in Christ, we were struggling.

We had just welcomed our second son, and Monica and I were arguing and fighting about everything. She was also facing an unnamed mental illness we can now identify as postpartum depression, and I was oblivious to her needs. I was also completely in over my head being a dad. I didn't know how to handle a two-year-old and a colicky newborn. I didn't know what I was doing, but I knew I was doing it wrong. I spent most of my time oscillating between frustration with myself and frustration with my kids.

I wanted to serve my family better, but I didn't know how. And I was taking out that frustration on them. Monica, to her surprise, had married a very passive man. She married a man who loved his faith but didn't know how to take his devotion to Jesus and turn it into love for his family. She would urge me to help lighten her load at home, and I wouldn't. I didn't know where to start, I didn't know what she needed. My fear of failing had me trying to ignore the problems that were festering within our marriage, hoping they would go away.

I also didn't know how to balance loving, disciplining, and teaching my kids. As the boys grew older, and we were preparing to welcome Gianna into our lives, I was dreading being a dad to a daughter. I knew I needed to change something, but I was clueless as to where to begin. I begged God for an answer, but I wasn't prepared for Him to actually answer.

Stay-At-Home-Dad Life

In 2017, right around the time Gianna was born, Monica and I discerned career changes. I needed to pause my career and she needed to pursue teaching. In hindsight, it was one of the best decisions we ever made, and I credit where we are now as a family to the moment we made the switch.

I go into more detail on how being a stay-at-home-dad changed me on *TwoBecomeFamily.com*, but here are the highlights: first, it showed me all of the things Monica did on a daily basis and I learned to appreciate her *so* much more. Second, it taught me how to care for my young kids, and how to manage myself and my emotions while caring for THEIR EVERY SINGLE NEED EVERY MOMENT OF EVERY DAY.

Most importantly, being a stay-at-home-dad, changed my spiritual perspective on being a father and a husband. I had no clue how to lead my family. My faith didn't inform my vocation. And up until that point, they were mostly unrelated realities. I never had an example of holy leadership in family life. I didn't have a tangible concept of how a husband and father should lead, and what the fruit of holy family leadership should be. My time at home changed all of that.

My SAHD (stay-at-home-dad) life started with playdates in the park with the kids from our friend group, but that quickly evolved to daily mass every morning with them as well. My time at daily mass began to slowly form me into the leader my family needed. God slowly revealed to me the wounds that I was still carrying around, and how those wounds were preventing me from leading and loving my family as I ought.

It was during this time that I began reading the writings of St. John Paul the Great. I suddenly had a moment in the middle of my day where I could read for 30-40 minutes (some people call it nap time). Reading during nap time led to reading in the mornings and evenings. I couldn't get enough of his wisdom.

Eventually, I finished *Love and Responsibility*. Then I moved to reading *Man and Woman He Created Them: A Theology of the Body* for the first time. From there I began working through St. John Paul's Papal writings, and that's when God really laid it on.

As God was healing wounds and working through baggage from my past, I was still struggling with what a holy husband and father looked like. I wanted to take the work God was doing in me, and let it affect my daily life. That's when God gave me a tangible ideal to pursue:

> "Love for his wife as mother of their children and love for the children themselves are for the man the natural way of understanding and fulfilling his own fatherhood. [...], efforts must be made to restore socially the conviction that the place and task of the father in and for the family is of unique and irreplaceable importance. [...] In revealing and in reliving on earth the very fatherhood of God, a man is called upon to ensure the harmonious and united development of all the members of the family." (St. John Paul the Great, Familiaris Consortio)

There it was. That's what I was supposed to do as a father and husband. That's what I needed to pursue. But now that I had the ideal, I asked the question, "How do I get there?" How do I go from where I am to where I want to be in leading my family?

Guardian of the Redeemer

Reading *Familiaris Consortio* led me to reading St. John Paul's Apostolic Exhortation on St. Joseph

Redemptoris Custos or *Guardian of the Redeemer*. This was my first in depth introduction to Joseph. St. John Paul changed how I saw St. Joseph and how I saw my role as husband and father. Instead of seeing service of God as separate from my role as husband and father, St. Joseph's example showed me that it was through my role as husband and father that I was serving God. My vocation was the means in which I served the Lord.

As St. John Paul wrote,

> "St. Joseph was called by God to serve the person and mission of Jesus directly through the exercise of his fatherhood. […] The Gospels clearly describe the fatherly responsibility of Joseph toward Jesus. For salvation-which comes through the humanity of Jesus-is realized in actions which are an everyday part of family life." (St. John Paul the Great, Redemptoris Custos)

Learning this for the first time led to hours of meditating and contemplating St. Joseph's life and how he loved and led his family. My time in prayer with Joseph led to tangible ways I needed to change to love and lead my family better.

After finishing the Apostolic Exhortation, I consecrated, or entrusted, myself and my role as husband and father to Jesus through St. Joseph.

St. John Paul the Great encouraged consecration to St. Joseph over 30 years ago, and I am grateful I followed his recommendation. Entrusting myself to St. Joseph changed the way I loved my bride, loved my kids, and how I led my family. God filled my need for a guide in fatherhood by providing me His own earthly father.

Change of Plans

I began writing down my reflections and insights as I prayed through the Gospels and other Papal documents that focused on St. Joseph. My hope was to one day write a book about this devotion in order to help others discover what I did through devotion to St. Joseph. But as quickly as I found myself a stay-at-home-dad, I found myself thrust back into my old field of work on March 19th, 2019 (o the Feast of St. Joseph).

Returning to work paused my aspirations to write the book. But I continued to grow as a husband and father, and my consecration was bearing good fruit! There were, and still are, plenty of bumps in the road as I try to love and lead my family. But I know that if it wasn't for my time as a stay-at-home-dad, and the example and devotion to St. Joseph, I would not be the kind of husband and father I am today.

The Year of St. Joseph

Fast forward to December 2020. I was delighted to see that December 8, 2020 to December 8, 2021 was going to be a year entrusted to St. Joseph! This news was the nudge I needed to take my reflections and put them together in a book.

God brings new devotions to us to help guide us in our time of need. We find that God continues to communicate hope to His people through devotions like the Sacred Heart, Divine Mercy, and countless Marian apparitions. As our culture has shifted, we see the Church respond by bringing us this new devotion. In the last 150 years our Church has slowly begun increasing the prominence and devotion to Joseph.

This book is my own way of participating in the promotion of devotion to this great Saint. We could never have too many books and resources promoting devotion and consecration to Joseph. I pray more come after me because he is the Saint we need in our time.

Go To Joseph

What you'll find in the following pages comes from my own reflections during my time as a struggling father and husband. The soil that grew this book is all of my own personal struggles and shortcomings. Time after time, God has shown up in my moments of weakness and provided the grace necessary for me to continue to love and lead my family. I don't do it perfectly, but I'm trying, and I can promise you that His grace is sufficient.

This book is not specifically for husbands and fathers, but I believe it would be of great benefit to them. This book, and the devotion to St. Joseph, can be transformational for anyone. Because of St. Joseph, my love for Jesus, my devotion to Mary, and faithfulness to my family has increased tenfold. I believe God desires that for all of us. I pray this book is a blessing to you and your family as you pursue a deeper friendship with St. Joseph.

Renzo

Saint Joseph,
Pray for us!

Introduction to Consecration to St. Joseph

Consecration to St. Joseph isn't actually consecration to St. Joseph. Let me explain, what is typically referred to as consecration to St. Joseph, is actually consecration to Jesus *through* St. Joseph or consecration to St. Joseph for short.

To consecrate something means to set it apart for a special purpose. When we consecrate ourselves, we are setting ourselves apart for Jesus Christ and His purposes. When we consecrate ourselves to Jesus *through* a saint (like Mary or St. Joseph) we are setting ourselves apart, for Christ, under the protection, guidance, and mentorship of either Mary or St. Joseph.

At the end of our 10 days together we will make an "Act of Consecration" and will be entrusting ourselves completely to Jesus under the patronage and protection of St. Joseph. For the rest of this book, we will be referring to this entrustment to Jesus through St. Joseph as consecration to St. Joseph.

Once we are consecrated, under the protection, guidance, and mentorship of St. Joseph, our devotion to St. Joseph will grow. As we grow, we will find that our hearts will begin to transform into a heart more like St. Joseph's. With this new heart, we can love and serve our Lord just like St. Joseph did.

Prepare Your Heart

God's invitation to consecration is an invitation to deeper conversion. God is inviting you and He is waiting for your response. But before you respond you must prepare. This short book will guide you in your preparation to respond to God so you can consecrate yourself to St. Joseph!

In the following chapters, we are going to use the Gospels to illustrate who St. Joseph was and learn how to go to Joseph. We are going to take excerpts from the Gospel and try to see St. Joseph through the eyes of those whom he loved the most: Mary and Jesus. Then we will reflect on what the Gospel is telling us about St. Joseph's role in our own spiritual lives.

As we learn more about the man, we will learn more about his heart and his virtue. As we grow to understand the depth of love that flowed from St. Joseph's heart, we will be drawn deeper into God's invitation of conversion. God desires deeper devotion and intimacy with us, and it is through St. Joseph's life, virtue, and example that Our Lord will draw us closer to Himself.

Fatherly Protection

During our preparation for consecration, we are also preparing ourselves to accept St. Joseph as our patron, spiritual provider, and protector. After our consecration, St. Joseph will be our patron in the sense that we will maintain a special relationship and devotion to him. He will no longer be a stranger, but a spiritual father to whom we can run to in times of need.

He will be our spiritual provider, because we will recourse to him and his intercession when we need the grace to persevere. Lastly, St. Joseph will be our protector.

St. Joseph will fight for us in moments of spiritual attack and temptation and will provide the same fatherly protection he provided Jesus. The protection of Christ did not end for Joseph. Now in

Heaven, St. Joseph is tasked with protecting and providing for us, the Church.

We, the Church, are part of Christ's body. And that body is the same body St. Joseph was tasked to protect and provide for since its conception. That is why St. Joseph desires to protect you as his own.

In fact, the virtues that St. Joseph modeled are the virtues he will defend within our own spiritual lives. By his protection, he will intercede for us in moments of hardship and struggle so that God will provide the graces necessary to excel in virtue. As he protects us and our virtue, we will be able to model his love of Christ more and more every day.

Our Model

In St. Joseph, God has given us a model of holiness that is accessible to everyone. Holiness can be intimidating if we see it as more things to do. We also don't need another holy person telling us the newest prayers, tips, and tricks to be more holy. Instead of special holiness hacks, what if there was a way to grow in holiness by doing the things we already have to do everyday? What if we can find holiness in our own homes? For that kind of holiness, St. Joseph is the perfect model for all of us.

As we'll read in the Gospels, St. Joseph's actions seem so ordinary that most of us forget how dynamic his part in salvation history was. The way he served God by being a father, husband, and worker, was extraordinarily ordinary!

St. Joseph didn't have to travel and preach, he didn't enlist and fight, he didn't march and conquer. St. Joseph simply cared for his family and worked everyday. He was like us. Wherever we are in our journey to Heaven, we can learn to love our parents, our children, our neighbors, and families better, just as St. Joseph did.

St. Joseph possesses an ongoing relevance to all the faithful striving and struggling to live out the universal call to holiness in their normal, everyday lives. In a culture where we're fed the lie that fame, followers, and influence equal success, we can too easily seek Christian influence more than Jesus Himself. That is why the life of St. Joseph flies directly in the face of cultural norms. In St. Joseph we find a life well lived for God. In him we'll find a model that we can follow.

Necessary Devotion

You might be wondering if this consecration is necessary to live a holy life. In order to answer that, we should first consider St. Joseph's role in salvation.

There are no recorded words of Joseph in the Gospels. Individually, he is not the central focus of the Gospel story. We don't hear much about the man, Joseph of Nazareth, beyond where he is mentioned in reference to Jesus or Mary. But the Story would not have unfolded without him; he was necessary. And he is still necessary. He was necessary for Jesus and Mary. He was necessary for the Gospel. He is necessary for our own spiritual lives.

It sounds blasphemous to say anyone other than Jesus is necessary With an omnipotent, all-powerful God, nothing is really necessary. God can do anything without needing anyone. That is why it is correct to say that consecration to St. Joseph is not necessary. In fact, consecration to Mary is not necessary, and the Incarnation of Jesus Christ, God becoming man, *was not necessary*.

The Incarnation, the Word becoming flesh, baby Jesus, was actually not necessary for our salvation. God could have saved us any way He would have liked. St. Thomas Aquinas explains about the necessity of the Incarnation when he wrote that:

> "A thing is said to be necessary [...] in two ways. First, when the end cannot be without it; as food is necessary for the preservation of human life. Secondly, when the end is *attained better and more conveniently*, as a horse is necessary for a journey. In the first way it was not necessary that God should become incarnate for the restoration of human nature." (ST III, q. 1, a. 2, co. emphasis added)

God, because He is omnipotent, could have restored humanity by any other means, but He *chose* to take on flesh. He *chose* to enter into human history through a family. God *chose* the Incarnation. Jesus becoming man allowed for our salvation to be, in St. Thomas's words, attained better and more conveniently.

But it was not the only way it could have been done. Now, for our purposes, let's apply St. Thomas's second definition of necessity to our consecration to St. Joseph. God doesn't need Mary and He doesn't need St. Joseph, but He chose to use them. Mary is God's most desired way for us to reach Jesus. God desires to grow Jesus in our hearts through the hands of the Blessed Mother. God also chooses St. Joseph as the necessary guardian and protector of Jesus. We need consecration to St. Joseph because it is the better and more convenient path that God has chosen for us. God chose St. Joseph to protect Jesus and Mary...and what's good enough for Jesus and Mary is surely good enough for us.

Working Together

Though the Church has always recognized St. Joseph as a Saint and has always had devotion to him, we are starting to see a resurgence towards this devotion. It's almost as though this devotion was specifically meant for our times. Pope Saint John XXIII wrote about this reserved devotion in 1961 saying,

> "But Joseph, except for some slight sprinkling of references to him here and there in the writings of the Fathers, for long centuries remained in the background that was so typical of him, like a kind of ornamental detail in the overall picture of the Savior's life. It took time for devotion to him to go beyond those passing glances and take root in the hearts of the faithful, and then surge forth in the form of special prayers and of a profound sense of trust and confidence. The fervent joy of pouring forth these deepest feelings of the heart in so many impressive ways has been saved for modern times; and it gives us special pleasure to draw upon these treasures now for something quite pertinent and meaningful." (Pope Saint John XXIII, Le Voci)

The period of darkness and confusion we are living in is being met by God through the consecration to St. Joseph.

Now, by this consecration to St. Joseph we are not making him into another Mary. Marian consecration is different from Josephite consecration, in the same manner that Mary's role in the life of Christ was different from St. Joseph's role in the life of Christ.

In God's plan for Jesus there was no either-or. Jesus did not have to decide to either be under the mantle of Mary or the protection of St. Joseph. Jesus entrusted Himself to both. Similarly, we should not see the consecration to Mary and the consecration to St. Joseph as competing devotions. If God chose to entrust Himself and His Blessed Mother to the care and protection of Joseph, it follows that God would choose Mary and St. Joseph for all of His children!

Protected by St. Joseph

Mary and St. Joseph work together to bring us to Jesus. Mary is the surest and safest way to Jesus, and St. Joseph is the surest and safest protection on our journey to Heaven. St. Joseph played many roles in salvation, and we will spend much of the rest of this book reflecting on his large, though hidden, role in salvation history.

However, it is important to understand, first, how this consecration, entrustment, and devotion to St. Joseph fits in with our love for Jesus through Mary. Like true spouses and parents, their roles in our spiritual lives complement each other. Mary increases our love for Jesus, and St. Joseph protects our love for Jesus.

St. Josemaria Escriva had a saying that explained, in a single sentence, the Catholic devotion to Mary: "All with Peter to Jesus through Mary!" I believe in our time, the faithful must move forward "All with Peter, to Jesus, through, Mary protected by Joseph."

CONSECRATION CHART

Start of 10 Day Preparation	Feast Day	Consecration Day
December 16	Feast of Holy Spouses	December 27
March 8	Solemnity of St. Joseph, Spouse of the Blessed Virgin Mary	March 19
April 21	Memorial of St. Joseph the Worker	May 1
8th day of the month	Traditional day of the month for St. Joseph	19th day of the month
Sunday	Traditional day of the week for St. Joseph	Wednesday

It is customary to try to make your Act of Consecration on a Feast Day. Here is a chart that can help you select when you want to start your preparation so that your Consecration falls on a day that honors St. Joseph.

Preparation For Consecration

Day 1

"The book of the genealogy of Jesus Christ, the son of David, the son of Abraham [...] Jacob the father of Joseph, the husband of Mary, of whom Jesus was born, who is called Christ."

-Matthew 1:1,16

    Typically, I don't read the introduction to books. I am more of a jump-right-into-the-story type of person. I like the temporary disorientation that comes as I try to figure out the characters, relationships, and plot on my own. It's a little like when you try to build something without the directions.

    The Genealogy in the Gospel of Matthew is typically treated like an unnecessary introduction to Jesus Christ. We know Jesus is the main character, and so we skip over the long list of hard to pronounce names (I'm looking at you, Ammin'adab) in order to get to the Jesus part quicker.

But if we rush through the beginning, we run the risk of missing out on some foundational information. This genealogy meant something to Matthew and his audience. If it wasn't for that long list of names, the entire Gospel message would have fallen on deaf ears.

Old in New

As St Augustine puts it, "The New Testament is concealed in the Old, and the Old Testament is revealed in the New." In scriptural theology the concealing of the New in the Old is known as typology. This is the idea that the New Testament story is foreshadowed in the Old Testament through people or events.

For example, Moses can be seen as a type, or foreshadowing, of Jesus. When we read about Moses and the Ten Commandments, we are told that he went up a mountain (Ex 19:3) and returned with a new law for God's people (Ex 19:25-20:1-17). In Matthew, we can see the parallel between Jesus and Moses.

Jesus saw the crowds following Him and, "went up on the mountain" (Mt 5:1). He brings about a new teaching to the point that, "The crowds were astonished at his teaching, for he taught them as one who had authority, and not as their scribes" (Mt 7:28-29). Moses is a type, or foreshadowing, of Jesus, and Jesus is the new Moses. And this new Moses brings a new law, to bring about a new exodus (Lk 4:18).

The foreshadowing of New Testament events isn't limited to the foreshadowing of the person of Jesus. There is also a foreshadowing of the important people around Him: Mary and St. Joseph. Mary is foreshadowed in many ways in the Old Testament. For example, the Church has often made parallels between Mary and Eve, calling Mary the "New Eve."

A lesser understood, but important parallel is between Mary and the Ark of the Covenant. Here is where we can also find a parallel for Joseph and King David.

God-Bearer

We can read more about the Ark of the Covenant in Exodus 25. Approximately one year after the Israelite's exodus from Egypt, the Ark was created. The Ark held the two tablets of the Ten Commandments, Aaron's rod, and manna (Heb 9:4). From above Ark, God spoke with Moses (Ex 25:22). The Ark is mentioned throughout the Old Testament story and travels with the Israelites. But the obvious parallels with Mary come in during the days of King David:

> "So David and all the house of Israel **brought up the ark of the LORD with shouting**, and with the sound of the horn." -2 Sm 6:15

> "**and she exclaimed with a loud cry**, "Blessed are you among women, and blessed is the fruit of your womb!" -Lk 1:42

> "As the ark of the LORD came into the city of David, Michal, daughter of Saul looked out of the window, and **saw King David leaping and dancing before the LORD**." -2 Sm 6:16A

> "For behold, when the voice of your greeting came to my ears, **the child in my womb leaped for joy**." -Lk 1:44

> "So David was not willing to take the ark of the LORD into the city of David; but David

took it aside to the house of O'bed-e'dom the Gittite. **And the ark of the LORD remained in the house of O'bed-e'dom the Gittite three months.**"
-2 Sm 6:10-11

"In those days Mary arose and went with haste into the hill country, to a city of Judah, [...] **And Mary remained with her about three months.**" (Lk 1:39,56)

The Ark of the Covenant bore God's presence and His holiness in the Old Testament. This was a foreshadowing of Mary's much more real bearing of God's presence to the world!

New David

Just as Jesus and Mary's roles were concealed in the Old Testament, it shouldn't be surprising that St. Joseph's role is also foreshadowed in the Old. Just like when Mary's foreshadowing as the *New* Ark of the Covenant becomes more obvious in the story of King David, St. Joseph's foreshadowing is also made present through King David.

David is typically, and rightly, thought of as a type of Christ, just like Moses. He is also a type of Joseph. David, and the Davidic line, was entrusted with the Ark. However, the Ark was lost during the Babylonian conquest, and the Davidic line failed to protect the Ark of God, until St. Joseph. It is through St. Joseph that the protection of the Ark by the Davidic line is complete because he was a descendent of King David.

For the rest of this book, we will consider the different ways that St. Joseph loved and cared for Mary and Jesus. As we walk through St. Joseph's life as depicted in the New Testament, we need to keep the lens of the Old Testament in our minds. St. Joseph is fulfilling the duties of the Davidic line, through his protection of the New Ark: Mary. In this way, during the first part of Christ's life, St. Joseph acts as a *new* David.

Though Jesus more perfectly fulfills the role of the new David, St. Joseph ushered in the entire Old Testament into the New as an heir to the Davidic line. St. Joseph acted as a new David and handed the lineage to Jesus to bring the duties of the King to fruition.

King Jesus

This typology wasn't lost on Matthew. God was intricately bringing together the whole story, from the beginning, and the culmination was going to be His Beloved Son.

Matthew's Gospel opens by tracing back Christ's genealogy from Abraham to Jesus (Mt 1), and Luke's Gospel traces from Adam to Jesus (Lk 3). Both evangelists bring past Jewish history and human history into focus as God becomes part of history Himself.

Matthew wrote for a Jewish audience, so he aimed to emphasize that Jesus was the Messiah that the Jews were awaiting. Luke, on the other hand, wrote for a Gentile audience and emphasized that Jesus was the savior the world was seeking.

To the evangelists there was no more important story to tell. But specifically, for Matthew, there was no more important detail than the fact that Jesus was a descendent of Abraham through the kingly Davidic line.

And how did God bring in the bloodline of Abraham and King David to Jesus? He did this through St. Joseph.

By having Jesus inherit this lineage, God seamlessly brings the past stories of the Old Testament into the New Testament. God had a plan from the Garden, and He made a promise to Abraham. In Jesus, through St. Joseph, God is making good on His promise.

Therefore, it's St. Joseph's involvement, his presence in the story, that legally endows Jesus with the kingly Davidic line that can be traced back to Abraham.

Jesus is fully God by His nature, fully human by Mary, and the rightful king by St. Joseph. It is by Mary that Christ receives His human nature, and it is by St. Joseph that He receives His human ancestry.

Go To Joseph

For our first day, let's go to Joseph and consider how God used him to weave together the stories of the Old and New Testaments. St. Joseph had a small role to play in a much grander drama that began long before he took Mary into his home.

God is a masterful author. He intricately intertwined the lives of many different individuals to bring us the perfect love story. The story didn't end after Christ's resurrection. We have our own role in this story. God has desired that we live during this time in human history for a purpose. Just as Joseph was chosen to fulfill a small yet vital role in salvation, God has chosen us as well.

As we move through this preparation for consecration, let God show you in what ways He desires you to serve, grow and love. Your impact may seem insignificant, but just like Joseph, you are a part of a much larger story. Strive to fulfill your role well.

Pause & Pray

Blessed St. Joseph,
Renowned offspring of David,
and Light of Patriarchs,
Increase your presence in my life.
By your intercession may I receive the grace to
hear and accept my calling.
Amen.

Day 2

"In the sixth month the angel Gabriel was sent from God to a city of Galilee called Nazareth, to a virgin betrothed to a man whose name was Joseph, of the house of David; and the virgin's name was Mary."
-Luke 1:26-27

When the Gospel of Luke recounts how Mary accepted her role in salvation history her role is obviously a major focal point of the story. Without Mary's "Yes" to the angel, the story never happens. It is through Mary that God chooses to enter into our world. She was a central figure in the story of salvation and remains a central figure in our own salvation.

But sometimes, when we are focused on Mary, we run the risk of forgetting Joseph. Like the opening verses in Matthew's account, it's easy to miss St. Joseph's role in Luke's account because it's eclipsed by Mary's much larger role.

That is not how the Gospel is written, however. Luke does not forget St. Joseph. As we read, we can notice that even though Luke's focus is on Mary, he makes sure to mention St. Joseph. Luke recognizes that St. Joseph is significant and wants his readers to know that too.

As Catholics, we believe that Mary was specifically chosen to be the Mother of Christ. We know that is why Mary was Immaculately Conceived without Original Sin. God preserved her from the moment of her conception and prepared her for this most important role.

But in a similar manner, God specifically chose St. Joseph to be the earthly father of Jesus, and the chosen spouse for Mary. For this reason, we should try to view Mary and St. Joseph side by side as true spouses. God did not focus on one and not the other. God chose them both. He had specific reasons for choosing Mary to be the Blessed Mother and St. Joseph to be the foster-father.

By spending time with both Mary and Joseph, we can learn more about the virtues that God values and desires in each of us.

Presence and Protection

God chose St. Joseph to fulfill many roles in the lives of Mary and Jesus, and early in the Gospels we can see that one of those roles is protector.

St. Joseph was the protector of the Holy Family.
That does not mean that the Gospels recount St. Joseph physically fighting anyone who was trying to hurt Jesus and Mary (I'm personally confident that he would have, if necessary). What it does mean is that protector was his designated role given to him by God.

Without knowing it, St. Joseph was protecting Mary and Jesus simply by his presence. If God had not brought Joseph into the picture when

He did, Mary would not have had anyone to support her and her newly conceived baby. Our Lady would have been sentenced to endure her pregnancy in complete isolation from her family, friends, and entire community (Dt 23:2). If it weren't for the fact that she was married to Joseph, Mary would have been cast out. Being an unmarried young woman, Mary would have had to carry the Savior of the world completely alone.

St. Joseph's presence kept Mary from experiencing a pregnancy filled with suspicion, slander, and isolation. Mary may not have been able to survive the pregnancy if Joseph was not in the picture.

The magnitude of God's decision to use St. Joseph affirms how integral his role of protector was in the salvation story. And as we'll see in the upcoming days, his role of protector didn't stop there. St. Joseph may not have been cast with spoken lines, but if he wasn't there, the whole story would have been different.

Go To Joseph

In the same way that St. Joseph affected salvation history by his presence, he can affect your spiritual life by his presence. Like with Mary, his presence will bring comfort and protection.

As you to begin to pray with St. Joseph, consider how Joseph's presence brought comfort to the child Jesus. Consider how protected the Holy Family felt under Joseph's care. And ask St. Joseph to bring that same comfort and protection into your life.

In moments of trial and temptation, go to Joseph and let him be a part of your preparation, comfort, and protection.

Pause & Pray

Blessed St. Joseph,
Spouse of the Mother of God,
Increase your presence in my life.
By your intercession, may I receive the grace to
trust in God's plan and to experience your presence
and protection in my life.
Amen.

Day 3

"And Mary said to the angel, "How can this be, since I have no husband?" And the angel said to her, "The Holy Spirit will come upon you, and the power of the Most High will overshadow you; therefore the child to be born will be called holy, the Son of God."

-Luke 1:34-35

Mary and St. Joseph had not consummated their marriage prior to the Annunciation. In his Apostolic Exhortation, *Redemptoris Custos*, Pope St. John Paul the Great tells us that,

> "According to Jewish custom, marriage took place in two stages: first, the legal, or true marriage was celebrated, and then, only after a certain period of time, the husband brought the wife into his own house."

At this point in the Christmas story, Mary and Joseph were legally married, but St. Joseph had not completed the Jewish marriage custom. Just like marriage customs in our time, there were rituals that those getting married had to go through before the marriage was considered complete.

After their legal marriage, according to Jewish custom, St. Joseph was to go build and prepare a place for his bride, then return and take her to that place (This type of language should sound familiar to us if we've ever read Jn 14:3, but that's for another book).

St. Joseph had not taken his bride into his home, so their marriage was still incomplete. It's in the home where the marriage would be consummated. And it's during the first stage of their marriage that the angel appears to Mary and Christ is conceived. It is also during this stage of their marriage that St. Joseph learns that Mary is with child.

The Just Man

As St. Joseph became aware of Mary's pregnancy, he had to reconcile the reality that they had not consummated their marriage.

Luke doesn't give us insight into the private conversations surrounding the God-planned pregnancy, but we are given insight into how St. Joseph acts in response to the news in the Gospel of Matthew.

In Matthew we read that, "Joseph, her husband, since he was a just man, yet unwilling to expose her to shame, decided to divorce her quietly" (Mt 1:16). Though we may not know what Mary said to Joseph regarding her pregnancy, we can assume from Joseph's action that he was either moving from a place of suspicion or fear.

When Mary tells St. Joseph that she conceived by the Holy Spirit, it's natural to assume that Joseph received this news suspiciously. None of us can fault St. Joseph for his very human response to Christ's conception. Leaning towards suspicion of Mary's good news, and assuming adultery, it makes sense that he would want to end the marriage. If Mary had been unfaithful, St. Joseph would have been within his right to let the full weight of divorce fall on Mary. Any Jewish man in that time would have done this. But because St. Joseph isn't just any man we can start to see why God chose him for such a huge role in salvation history.

St. Joseph takes his divorce request a step further and decides to carry out the divorce quietly in order to preserve Mary's dignity. Instead of a public rebuke and demonstration, St. Joseph opted to do as little damage as possible to Mary's reputation and future. Joseph preserved Mary's dignity when Jewish law claimed she no longer had any.

Jewish law of that time was clear, "If a man commits adultery with his neighbor's wife, both the adulterer and the adulteress shall be put to death" (Lev 20:10).

You Have Heard That It Was Said

St. Joseph was well within his right, according to Jewish law, to shame the Blessed Mother and to stone her. But in this moment, we can see that God is beginning to work something new. The new Law that Jesus is to give one day during His Sermon on the Mount is prefigured here through His foster-father's actions.

In the recounting of the Sermon, Matthew quotes Jesus elevating the Law to a seemingly unreachable standard. He does this using the phrase, "You have heard that it was said, but I say to you…" For example:

"You have heard that it was said, 'An eye for an eye and a tooth for a tooth.' But I say to you, Do not resist one who is evil. But if anyone strikes you on your right cheek, turn to him the other also." (Mt 5:38-39)

Or

"You have heard that it was said, 'You shall love your neighbor and hate your enemy.' But I say to you, Love your enemies, and pray for those who persecute you." (Mt 5:43-44)

St. Joseph's actions after finding out about Mary's pregnancy is a manifestation of what Christ would teach 33 years later. St. Joseph had heard that it was said to stone the adulteress, but God was saying something different to his heart. God was going to bring about a new message of mercy through the life of Jesus, and He started this message through Joseph's actions. God showed the world mercy through Joseph before He showed mercy through Jesus.

Go To Joseph

Go to Joseph to learn mercy. The heart of St. Joseph raised the Merciful and Sacred Heart of Jesus. God, in all His Divine wisdom, made sure that Jesus would be fathered by the merciful heart of St. Joseph.

Consider for a moment those who have wronged you, or those you perceived have wronged you in some manner. Being merciful towards the weaknesses and shortcomings of those around us is difficult. We tend to judge others by a perfectionistic scale to which they will always fall short. What's worse is that we tend to judge ourselves by that scale as well.

Through St. Joseph's actions we see mercy at work. Reflect on his example. Allow the Lord to soften your heart so that you can learn to forgive others more readily, and yourself more frequently. If you haven't been to confession in a while, make an appointment to go during this preparation and experience the mercy of God firsthand.

Pause & Pray

Blessed St. Joseph,
Chaste Guardian of the Virgin
Increase your presence in my life.
By your intercession may I receive the grace to forgive others more readily and myself more frequently, increase my love for Christ found in the Sacrament of Reconciliation.
Amen.

Day 4

"But as he considered this, behold, an angel of the Lord appeared to him in a dream, saying, "Joseph, son of David, do not fear to take Mary your wife, for that which is conceived in her is of the Holy Spirit.'"

-Matthew 1:20

There is another way to look at St. Joseph's attempt to divorce Mary quietly, and it is worth considering as we grow in friendship with this faith filled Saint.

In his commentary on the Gospel of Matthew, St. Thomas Aquinas notes that, "According to Jerome and Origen, he (Joseph) had no suspicion of adultery" (Aquinas, *Commentary on the Gospel of St. Matthew*). The alternative to the belief that St. Joseph reacted with suspicion at Mary's news is the belief that St. Joseph acted, from what I'd call, a place of fear and unworthiness.

If we examine what St. Thomas mentions here, we learn that the alternative proposes that St. Joseph learned that Mary had conceived of the Holy

Spirit and believed her. St. Joseph would have been familiar with the prophecy and with Mary's holiness. He would have learned of the miracle of Christ's conception and praised God for His mighty work.

But Joseph's thought then turned inward. And as St. Thomas says, "And so, considering himself unworthy to live together with such holiness, he wanted to put her away secretly; just as Peter said: "Depart from me, O Lord, for I am a sinful man" Lk 5:8" (Aquinas, *Commentary on the Gospel of St. Matthew*).

St. Joseph would have seen the magnitude of the role that God was calling him to and concluded that he was not worthy, and that is what moved him to divorce Mary quietly. And from this place of unworthiness God grew unshakable faith.

Fiat

While St. Joseph moves forward to quietly divorce the Blessed Mother, God intervenes through an angel and tells St. Joseph to take Mary into his home. This was St. Joseph's *Fiat* moment.

In Catholic circles, the word Fiat (pronounced FEE + UHT) typically refers to Mary's response to the angel during the Annunciation. At the Annunciation, the angel appears to Mary with news that she will conceive the Savior in her womb and Mary replies,

> "Let it be done to me according to your word." (Lk 1:38)

In Latin, that verse is translated to "Fiat mihi secundum verbum tuum et." Fiat is also a word God uses in Genesis 1:3 when He says, "Let there be light" or in Latin, "Fiat lux."

The Fiat from Mary was heroic because of how earth-shattering the words of the angel were. For Mary to receive such powerful news and in turn, equally trust in the providence of God shows why she is honored above all Saints. St. John Paul preached about how disruptive God's words by the angel were in a homily when he said that,

> "The divine promise comes as something completely unexpected. God disrupts the daily course of [life], overturning its settled rhythms and conventional expectations." (Homily March 25, 2000)

And the disruptive news was exclusively for Mary. God had His own set of disruptive news for St. Joseph and this ushered in his own "Let it be done" moment.

This is another case where Mary and St. Joseph must be contemplated side by side as true spouses. As we consider how God is working in both their lives, we will see how their situations are foreshadowing what their Son will endure in the future. Both Mary and St. Joseph's "Fiat" moments would eventually culminate in a similar moment for Christ, "Not my will but yours be done" (Lk 22:42). Each "Yes" to God gave way to another "Yes." Each disruption and Fiat was necessary for our salvation.

Annunciations

When the angel appeared to him in a dream, St. Joseph did not have to go along with God's plan. In his freedom, Joseph could have taken the news from the dream, and decided that it was too much to handle. God was asking the unthinkable of him.

Not only was he being asked to take Mary into his home, even though she was pregnant with a child that was not his, he was also expected to believe that the child was conceived through the power of the Holy Spirit!

No one would have blamed him for sneaking away after this, in the same way that no one could have blamed Mary for refusing the news from the angel that she would bear God's Son. St. John Paul points out how similar Mary and St. Joseph's "Annunciations" are:

> "There is a strict parallel between the "annunciation" in Matthew's text and the one in Luke. The divine messenger introduces Joseph to the mystery of Mary's motherhood. While remaining a virgin, she who by law is his "spouse" has become a mother through the power of the Holy Spirit. And when the Son in Mary's womb comes into the world, he must receive the name Jesus." (Redemptoris Custos, 3)

Mary and St. Joseph both had Annunciation moments, and both had Fiat moments. But how they give God their Fiat is completely unique.

In Mary, we find one of the most beautiful responses ever given to God. Her "Yes" has become an antiphon of the faithful who want to emulate docility to the will of God in the midst of seemingly impossible situations.

In St. Joseph we find a response that is just as powerful, but quiet. Like all of Joseph's responses to God, his "Yes," his Fiat, does not come in words, but through action.

> "When Joseph awoke, he did as the angel of the Lord had commanded him and took his wife into his home." (Mt 1:24)

St. Joseph's action is an embodiment of Mary's words. One Fiat sheds light on the other. When reading these stories side by side we are privy to the complementarity of spouses within the Holy Family.

Go To Joseph

Go to Joseph and ask him to teach you how you can best respond to the promptings of the Holy Spirit in your life.

As followers of Jesus we will have many Annunciations moments. Though they may never be of the magnitude of Mary and Joseph's, there will a time when God's will enters our lives and completely disrupts our "settled rhythms and conventional expectations."

How will you respond? Go to Joseph so that he can teach you how to respond to God's Annunciations with your own Fiat. Sometimes, God asks and we are left speechless and feeling unworthy.

With Joseph we see that even when we don't believe that we are capable, we can trust that God will provide where we lack. And even if we are lost for words, we can still respond to God by actions. Through this consecration may we learn that when God calls we must always choose to act.

Pause & Pray

Blessed St. Joseph,
Head of the Holy Family
Increase your presence in my life.
By your intercession may I receive the grace to
Act on the commands of the Lord with unwavering
confidence in His goodness.
Amen.

Day 5

"Now when they had departed, behold, an angel of the Lord appeared to Joseph in a dream and said, "Rise, take the child and his mother, and flee to Egypt, and remain there until I tell you; for Herod is about to search for the child to destroy him. And he rose and took the child and his mother by night and departed for Egypt."

-Matthew 2:13-14

    St. Joseph lived his familial vocation anchored in a deeply obedient faith in God. We saw that in yesterday's reading and reflection and today we read it again.

    After Christ's birth, and the visit of the Magi, the angel appears to St. Joseph again. This time the angel commands him to go to Egypt in order to escape Herod.

    Without hesitation, St. Joseph brings Jesus and Mary to Egypt under the cover of night. Another Annunciation moment is met with an unwavering

Fiat from St. Joseph. And this Fiat is why some have referred to St. Joseph as the "savior of our Savior."

When we read Joseph's quick action as a response to God's command, we must be careful to assume that it came easily to Joseph. There couldn't have been anything easy about what they were going to do. Imagine a newborn Jesus and a postpartum Mary suddenly whisked away by St. Joseph because an angel talked to him in a dream again!

Once again they are disrupted from their settled rhythms and expectations. They thought they were going to Bethlehem for a simple census, and now they're running away from a king who wants to kill their baby. What could have been worse? Well, if we read through the text again, we'll discover that the command to flee to Egypt was even more difficult than what we imagined.

Uprooted

The Holy Family wasn't just switching gears from one move (Nazareth to Bethlehem) to the next move (Bethlehem to Egypt). If we consider the scriptures, we can see that they weren't coming to Egypt right after Christ's birth. The Holy Family was being uprooted at least a year after Christmas day.

When the Magi are introduced into the story, we find them meeting with king Herod and asking,

> "Where is he who *has been born king of the Jews*? For we have seen his star in the East, and have come to worship him." (Mt 2:2, emphasis added)

They don't ask for a newborn king, but he who has been born. To this Herod requests to know where and when the star appeared. (Mt 2:4, 2:7). The star was no longer visible by this time, which is why the

Magi went to Herod to inquire Christ's location. That means, by the time the Magi found Jesus, He could have been anywhere, not necessarily Bethlehem. It's doubtful St. Joseph and Mary wanted to stick around the manger (Lk 2:7). It is more likely that the Holy Family returned to Nazareth in Galilee after the completion of the census.

Herod would not have known where Christ was, or how old He was. That is why:

> "When Herod realized that he had been deceived by the magi, he became furious. He ordered the massacre of all the boys in Bethlehem and its vicinity *two years old* and under, in accordance with the time he had ascertained from the magi." (Mt 2:16, emphasis added)

If Herod ordered the massacre of all two-year-olds, it's probable that at least a year had passed since the star appeared.

Obedience in Uncertainty

The historical background of the events in the Gospels emphasizes just how much God was asking of St. Joseph when the angel appeared. Mary and St. Joseph had already begun making a life in Nazareth. They had already presented Jesus in the temple in Jerusalem (Lk 2:21-38) and were living surrounded by friends and family. St. Joseph had established steady work to provide for his family, to provide for God's Son and God's mother.

Through this lens, we can see that to be asked to move to a completely foreign land, where Jews were once slaves, seems preposterous.

This is proof that God knew who He was putting in charge of His most beloved treasures. God placed St. Joseph as the head of the Holy Family precisely because of the type of man he was and the virtue he possessed. Instead of arguing, debating, hiding, or pleading with God, St. Joseph *obeyed*.

In St. Joseph's act of obedience, we can see his humility come to light. A father's impulse would typically be to stand, fight, and protect. He could have presented an alternative plan to God, one that did not include uprooting his family from everything they knew. But instead, in his usual silence, St. Joseph took the path of humility and trusted the Lord's command.

Go To Joseph

Go to Joseph to learn obedience in uncertainty. Typically, faithful obedience is easier when the circumstances and outcomes are certain. It's much easier following God when we have some sort of idea how things will turn out. But rarely does God call us to a life of certainty. He does not illuminate our entire path from now until Heaven.

Instead, God illuminates a single step and asks us to follow. With each step we take, we can see one more step ahead. We will never see the whole picture.

Go to Joseph to learn to rest on God's providence more than your own certainty. Contemplate what it took for Joseph to move in uncertainty. He did not know how he was to fulfill the vocation God had given him, but he trusted that if God was calling, God would also provide.

With St. Joseph, consider ways that God is calling you to move for Him. God may not be calling you to completely uproot your family, but He may be calling you into a discomfort that feels like uprooting. He may be calling you out of a situation, a relationship, or a behavior.

When God calls us out of something, He is typically calling us towards something else. Are there Nazareths and Egypts in your life that you are refusing to respond to? Go to Joseph and ask him to show you how to trust.

Pause & Pray

Blessed St. Joseph,
Diligent protector of Christ,
Increase your presence in my life.
By your intercession may I receive the grace to
Respond to the Lord's prompting and commands
with obedience and trust.
Amen.

Day 6

"How can this be, since I have no husband?" -Luke 1:34

Another title that St. Joseph is known as is the Chaste Spouse of Mary. Besides his silence, his chastity is what he is most well-known for in Catholic circles.

At this point in our preparation, hopefully we have been able to uncover the powerful strength of faith and obedience that lay behind Joseph's silence. The more that we've gotten to know St. Joseph and meditate on his life, the more we should consider silence as an outward sign of a deep interior life. But his silence, the fact that there are no recorded words in the Gospels, are a result of what God wanted to convey to us through the Gospel authors. It doesn't mean that St. Joseph spent his days in complete silence.

St. Joseph lived in community with other people and lived in a family with Jesus and Mary. He must have spoken words the same as any other father, husband, and worker. However, we still have to contend with why there are no words of Joseph. I'm sure every believer would have loved to know with what tone and tenderness St. Joseph addressed Jesus and Mary with. Each word of his would have been perfect prayers to the Savior and the Blessed Mother. The Gospel writers, inspired by the Holy Spirit, maintained focus on his actions. That is because his actions were more important than his words. His actions revealed the man, more than his words could have. And because his actions provide us with a powerful model to emulate.

So today we consider St. Joseph's model of chastity that God has woven into the story of Salvation. St. Joseph's chastity is a powerful example that is often overlooked or misunderstood. As we'll read, his chastity was not out of weakness, impotence, or passivity. St. Joseph's chastity was an outward sign of his interior virtue. By putting his virtue on display, the Gospel authors show us St. Joseph as the exemplar of what effect the Redemption of Jesus Christ can have in our lives.

Young and Old

In the early years of the Church, we can see that St. Joseph is depicted as an older man. When St. Joseph was portrayed this way by artists, they weren't necessarily making a historical claim about Joseph's age, but rather they were making a more theological interpretation of Christ's "brothers" (Mk 6:3) and of Joseph's chastity in the Gospels. Unfortunately, as Venerable Fulton Sheen puts it, "Art thus unconsciously made Joseph a spouse chaste and pure by age rather than by virtue" (Sheen, The World's First Love, 7).

The theory that St. Joseph must have been an older man derives from the idea that Joseph was a widower and Christ's "brothers" (Mt 13:55) were from a previous marriage. Therefore, God had chosen an older man to be the Chaste Spouse of Mary.

The thinking was that God chose an older Joseph because he would not have experienced the sexual desire, drive, or urge, to the same magnitude as a more virile, younger man would. Having tempered desires would have certainly made it easier for Joseph to guard Mary's virginity. Hence, some scholars and theologians conclude that St. Joseph must have been older in order to remain chaste for the entirety of his marriage. If this is true, it is no reason to praise St. Joseph. Like Fulton Sheen poignantly points out, "To make Joseph appear pure only because his flesh had aged is like glorifying a mountain stream that has dried." (Sheen, The World's First Love, 7).

It's evident in the Gospels that Christ's "brothers" were not familial brothers, but rather cousins or close relatives (Mk15:40). The two verses in Mark show that the supposed "brothers" of Jesus belonged to a different woman named Mary, demonstrating they were not directly the offspring of Mary or St. Joseph.

Furthermore, an older portrayal of St. Joseph takes away from the powerful model of chastity that he is. The belief that Joseph's age explains how Joseph was chaste, can lead us to incorrectly conclude that chastity is only possible through biological restriction rather than virtue.

As the faithful have developed and deepened their understanding of St. Joseph, another theory has become popularized. As scholars and theologians have come to consider the physical requirements that Joseph's life and work would have demanded, they have begun to portray Joseph as a younger, vibrant man.

Sanctified

With this new understanding, some theologians have theorized that St. Joseph must have received the grace to be chaste in the womb before his birth. This has been referred to as a sanctification in the womb. They believe that, as a result of this sanctification, St. Joseph did not have any disordered sexual desires that resulted from Original Sin, and therefore that's how he was able to remain chaste.

Like the old age portrayal of St. Joseph, this idea also falls short because it portrays chastity as a virtue that can only be achieved through passive reception of God's grace. This type of chastity is a result of God's grace but says nothing of Joseph's cooperation with grace.

Our Catholic faith tells us that disordered desires, or concupiscence, are a result of the fall of Adam and the inheritance of everyone who joins the human family.

The effects of the sanctification of St. Joseph couldn't have been a complete erasure of the broken human nature he inherited from Adam. St. Joseph was not Immaculately conceived like Mary. This theory, though well-meaning, takes away from the heroism St. Joseph lived. And, therefore, it dulls the vibrant example of chastity that we need in our culture today. In a world that struggles with chastity, St. Joseph is a sign of hope.

Transformed

St. Joseph was not a master of his desires because he lacked them in his old age. And his young virility was not tamed by a sanctification, likened to that of the Blessed Mothers Immaculate

Conception. St. Joseph fully possessed the energy, vitality, and impulses of a young man. It was Mary's love for him and his love for Mary that transformed Joseph into the most chaste spouse we honor!

> "A woman's love always determines the way a man loves: she is the silent educator of his virile powers. Since Mary is what might be called a "virginizer" of young men as well as women, and the greatest inspiration of Christian purity, should she not logically have begun by inspiring and virginizing the first youth whom she had probably ever met—Joseph, the Just? It was not by diminishing his power to love but by elevating it that she would have her first conquest, and in her own spouse, the man who was a *man*" (Sheen, The World's First Love, 7).

We may never know St. Joseph's true age this side of Heaven, but what we do know is that he possessed and exercised virtue.

St. Joseph's older portrayals are accurate in that they show the full possession of temperance and prudence that is typically found in old age. St. Joseph's portrayals as a young man are accurate in that they express Joseph's possession of courage and justice through his actions. Every portrayal of St. Joseph shows an aspect of who this man was. No single painting or statue could fully express all the interior virtue he possessed.

No matter how many swords or flowers we have him hold, we can never fully convey how transformed this man was after he looked in the Blessed Mother's eyes and held the newborn Christ in his arms.

Free To Love

This is where St. Joseph's model to us shines. His example to us is the most accessible out of all three members of the Holy Family. He is not the Savior of the world, or the Immaculate Conception. St. Joseph was an ordinary man, who possessed extraordinary virtue and holiness. That means we can be like Joseph because he was just like us!

St. Joseph was able to exercise heroic chastity, because he possessed self-mastery. This self-mastery came as a result of his love for Mary. It is through Mary, that God worked to grow St. Joseph in virtue, and it is through Mary that God desires to work in us!

The work that God desires to do in us will result in, not only freedom from sin, but freedom to love! Joseph was able to love Mary because he was not controlled by his wants or desires. By God's grace, St. Joseph became master over all his human impulses and was free to love Mary as he ought. This is why Venerable Fulton Sheen could say that "No husband and wife ever loved one another so much as Joseph and Mary." (Sheen, *The World's First Love*). Chastity and freedom were the foundation of this love between the spouses of the Holy Family. The Chaste heart of St. Joseph burned for love for the Immaculate heart of Mary.

The Catechism of the Catholic Church tells us that, "Chastity includes an *apprenticeship in self-mastery* which is a training in human freedom" (Catechism of the Catholic Church, 2339 emphasis added). St. Joseph is the shining example of what self-mastery and human freedom look like, and we can start following his example by going to Mary!

Go To Joseph

Go to Joseph today and pray the Rosary with him. Ask that Mary's love for you transform your heart so that you can desire to love her and Jesus as St. Joseph did. This desire to love will be the catalyst that will begin God's great work in us.

This does not mean that living our virtue is easy, Love does not take away our burdens, but instead gives us a reason to bare them courageously. Look to Joseph to show you what that looks like in your life. There are days when living out our holiness comes easy, and there are days when living out our holiness is nearly impossible.

Go to Joseph so he can show you what he did on those hard days. To say St. Joseph was chaste or possessed self-mastery is not to say that Joseph never struggled. There were times when St. Joseph didn't want to get up early to work, there were times when Joseph didn't want to do another project, and there were times when St. Joseph would have, perhaps for only a moment, longed to be one with his bride. But virtue and holiness does not mean the absence of struggle. Our struggle is the precursor to virtue; it is precisely in the hard moments that God showers us with His grace and gives us the strength to act.

Those moments of St. Joseph were fleeting because he was a man predisposed to cooperation with grace. Go to Joseph and let him show you how to cooperate with the grace God wants to pour out into your heart this day.

Pause & Pray

Blessed St. Joseph,
Guardian of virgins,
Increase your presence in my life.
By your intercession may I receive the grace to
grow in holiness through my struggles.
Amen.

Day 7

"[…] but knew her not until she had borne a son; and he called his name Jesus"

-Matthew 1:25

      If yesterday's reflection on St. Joseph's chastity left you uneasy, you're not alone. The idea of St. Joseph desiring Mary as his bride is not an image often portrayed. The fact remains that St. Joseph was madly in love with his bride, and it's that love for Mary that fueled his chastity.

      Mary's virginity was a gift she reserved for God alone. In protecting this gift, St. Joseph affirms how good sexuality is. If our sexuality wasn't a good thing, how could Mary offer it to God? Joseph was able to participate in the gift by protecting it for Mary.

      That does not mean that St. Joseph didn't desire to love his bride as a husband. Joseph's romantic love for Mary was passionate and vibrant and real. But his romantic love led him to a sacrificial love for her. Any romantic love, or romantic desire in our own lives, is supposed to lead us to a sacrificial love for the other. St. Joseph did experience desires that resulted from concupiscence, but the experience of concupiscence led him to a greater love.

Our Inheritance

There is a misconception in popular Christianity that equates the desire for sin with the committing of sin. The reason resisting or avoiding sin in our lives is so hard, is because sin is pleasing to the eyes (Gen 3:6). Our desire of sin emerges from the recognition that a particular thing is good. Some of the most powerful vices such as sex and alcohol at their essence possess a goodness. However, because of our concupiscence we see that goodness through a distorted lens.

Before Original Sin came what St. John Paul the Great called Original Man. Original Man, Adam and Eve, experienced life without the distorted lens we inherited. And because Original Man did not experience any of the effects of sin, he was completely free to love as he ought.

With the introduction of sin into the world came the disorder of our world, our human nature, and our desires. The human nature we know now:

> "is wounded in the natural powers proper to it, subject to ignorance, suffering and the dominion of death, and inclined to sin - an inclination to evil that is called *concupiscence.*" (Catechism of the Catholic Church, 405, emphasis added)

Because of Original Sin, our desires are disordered. That does not mean we have disorders, rather, it means that our desires are supposed to be ordered differently. Our lenses distort how we experience the world and lead us to find our satisfaction in things rather than God. That is sin: when our desires miss the mark, and attempt to be satisfied by something other than the One that could satisfy them.

Let There Be Freedom

When we experience desires as a result of our concupiscence, we are not sinning, because we cannot control experiencing them. The belief that concupiscence itself is a sin was introduced by the reformers of the sixteenth century. The protestant reformers, including Martin Luther, taught that:

> "Concupiscence is of itself sinful and being the sinful corruption of human nature caused by Adam's transgression and inherited by all his descendants, is the very essence of original sin." (The Catholic Encyclopedia)

This misunderstanding of concupiscence has led to a puritanical view of sexuality in western culture and has led to much hurt and confusion for those who are trying to live chastely. A lot of times the faithful equate freedom from sin and freedom from struggle. Through Christ we can experience freedom from sin, which gives us freedom *to* struggle. The struggle is not permanent, it is through the struggle that we will learn to rely on grace and be sanctified and redeemed.

The Good News of the Gospel is that we are not lost to concupiscence and sin. We are not slaves to our desires, and we can have true freedom. God has given us St. Joseph as a model of this freedom.

Theology of the Body

Our view of concupiscence as sinful, specifically the experience of sexual desires as sinful, comes from an incorrect understanding of concupiscence! That is why it was revolutionary to all of Christianity when Pope St. John Paul taught that,

> "Man is not responsible for what happens to him in the sphere of sex [...] since he is obviously not himself the cause of it, but he is entirely responsible for what he does in this sphere." (Love and Responsibility, 45)

St. John Paul acknowledged that we are incapable of controlling how we feel or what we desire, but we are free to choose how we *act*. That is how St. Joseph lived. That is what it means to be free.

This is why he was able to remain chaste in his marriage. By his virtue, St. Joseph was free to love as he ought. As St. John Paul writes in his epic work now known as the Theology of the Body:

> "The ethos of redemption is realized in self-mastery, by means of temperance, that is, continence of desires." (Theology of the Body 49:5)

Our self-mastery, realized through virtues like chastity, are a participation in the redemption Christ won for us and a small glimpse into the freedom we will experience in Heaven. That is the freedom that St. Joseph experienced on Earth, and the kind of freedom God desires to give you.

Go To Joseph

Go to Joseph today and let him show you how to live in the freedom Christ has purchased for you.

If you are married, do you live out the virtue of chastity in your marriage? Do you sacrifice and put your spouse first in all things as Joseph did?

If you are dating or engaged, are you living out chastity in your state in life? Are you placing the goodness and holiness of your beloved above your desires? Like St. Joseph, you have an opportunity to protect your beloved in order that they may grow closer to our Lord.

If you are single, are you striving for continued growth in areas of self-mastery like St. Joseph? Singleness is a tremendous opportunity to allow God to form you into the follower He desires without the distraction of relationships. Consider, in your singleness: are you loving those around you as you ought?

If you are someone who does not struggle with chastity, let God show you how else you can grow in temperance. Chastity falls under the virtue of temperance and in a culture driven by consumption, the struggle to exercise freedom through temperance is real.

Is our consumption of the things of this world ordered towards love of God and neighbor? By St. Joseph's example, let all that we do be directed for the good of others and of God. No matter our state in life, let us begin to live in the freedom to love as we ought.

Pause & Pray

Blessed St. Joseph,
Most prudent and Most chaste,
Increase your presence in my life.
By your intercession may I receive the grace to
grow in freedom and love as I ought.
Amen

Day 8

"And when they saw him they were astonished; and his mother said to him, "Son, why have you treated us so? Behold, your father and I have been looking anxiously." And he said to them, "How is it that you sought me? Did you not know that I must be in my Father's house?"

-Luke 2:48-49

      We can wonder how difficult it must have been for St. Joseph to raise a son who he knew wasn't biologically his own. We can meditate on how much harder it must have been for St. Joseph to raise a son who was also God incarnate.

      This short scene in Luke's Gospel portrays a particularly confusing moment in the lives of the Holy Family. Though Luke may not have given us many details about the Holy Family's interior life, we can appreciate a glimpse into one of their family meetings.

      The scene kicks off as young Jesus goes missing after the Holy Family had journeyed to Jerusalem for the Passover. After searching for

Jesus for three days, the evangelist recounts the Holy Family's interaction in Luke 2:48-49.

Notice Mary's words to Jesus, "Your father and I have been looking for you with great anxiety." Mary naturally, and rightfully refers to St. Joseph as Christ's father. To Mary's question, Jesus responds, "Did you not know that I must be in my Father's house?"

All three members of the Holy Family were aware of Christ's divinity. Notice how Jesus responds to Mary's inquiry, "Did you not know?" This phrase implies that Christ's relation to *The* Father was well known within the walls of the Holy Family's home.

Honor Your Father

The first time Jesus called anyone father wasn't when He taught His disciples how to pray (Mt 6:9-13) and it wasn't in Gethsemane as He begged the Father (Mk 14:6). The first time Jesus called anyone father would have been when He spoke to St. Joseph. In the middle of cooing and baby talk, Jesus would have looked at St. Joseph and called him Abba.

The relationship between St. Joseph and Jesus will remain shrouded in mystery this side of Heaven. We don't know the inner workings and dynamic between the members of the Holy Family, but we *do* know there was perfect love.

This perfect love extended from Jesus to Mary, and from Jesus to St Joseph. Jesus, being the complete fulfilment of the Law of God, would have perfectly loved and honored the man He first called father.

So we're still left with the question: if Christ did not mean to insult St. Joseph by His words, what did He mean?

Higher Power

Pope St. John Paul sheds a little light on this exchange during a homily he gave in 2001. In it St. John Paul tells us that,

"It is precisely these words of the Son that help
us to understand the mystery of Joseph's "fatherhood." In reminding his parents of the primacy of the One whom he called "my Father", Jesus reveals the truth about Mary's and Joseph's role." (Homily March 19, 2001)

Jesus was not saying that St. Joseph's role and relationship to Mary and Himself were false. And Jesus was also not trying to reprimand, embarrass, nor correct His Blessed Mother because she referred to St. Joseph as His father. Jesus was reminding them that St. Joseph's role of "husband and father is totally subordinate to that of God." (Pope St. John Paul the Great, Homily March 19, 2001)

Jesus was reminding them of His mission; like the reminder that Mary and St. Joseph were met with as they presented Jesus in the temple. In the temple Mary and St. Joseph were amazed at Simeon's words about Jesus. Simeon had waited his whole life to see the Messiah and what followed was an inspired prayer of hope (Lk 2:29-33), but Simeon also left Mary with a prophecy that must have shaken her and Joseph:

"Behold, this child is destined for the fall and rise of many in Israel, and to be a sign that will be contradicted, and you yourself a sword will pierce so that the thoughts of many hearts may be revealed."(Lk 2:34-35)

Did St. Joseph wonder why Simeon hadn't address him as well? Did St. Joseph think to himself how he would *never* let anything happen to Mary? And did those thoughts and memories come flooding back as Jesus reminded him that his fatherhood served a greater purpose than he could ever imagine?

St. Joseph had the almost impossible task of leading a family that was more perfect and holy than he could ever be. At the dinner table he sat next to God incarnate and the Immaculate Conception, yet he was designated the head. St. Joseph was the perfect man to lead Jesus and Mary, because he was a man that knew that in order to lead, you need to *serve*.

Following the Leader

In our culture, the idea of leadership has become warped and stripped of its truest meaning. As kids we are introduced to games like follow the leader, and learn, at a young age, that a leader does, and a follower is supposed to copy. This type of leadership is not how St. Joseph led his family.

The term "servant-leader" has grown in popularity because it correctly captures the essence of what leadership should look like. Leadership should be about the good of the other rather than for one's own benefit. Sounds a lot like love, right?

Jesus was the perfect example of a servant-leader because His entire mission was other-focused. He came *for* us. He did not come to be served, but to serve (Mt 20:28). Jesus feeds the hungry, heals the sick, washes the feet of the disciples, and carries His cross for *us*. Jesus led with love. And He first experienced this servant-leadership within His family from St. Joseph.

St. Joseph's leadership did not hinge on being smarter, mightier, or holier than Mary and Jesus, because he wasn't. St. Joseph's leadership hinged on the fact that he was the father and his duty was to love and serve his family!

St. Joseph fed the hungry, gave drink to the thirsty, and clothed the naked. He did not figuratively do it to others while thinking of Christ (Mt 25:35-36), St. Joseph did that for Jesus Himself. Joseph lived out the servant-leadership that Jesus later calls His own disciples to when He teaches them about the works of mercy. Through St. Joseph, Jesus experienced the works of mercy first in the home, acted out by the leader of His family.

That is why St. Joseph would not have been scandalized or disheartened with the reminder that his role of husband and father was subordinate to the Son he was tasked to raise. Instead, St. Joseph would have taken these as words of affirmation.

Go To Joseph

There are many situations in our lives when leading others is hard. There are even more situations where loving others is hard. Go to St. Joseph and ask him to show you how to love and lead as he did. Become a disciple of St. Joseph's discipleship.

Joseph led by serving, and in his service, he became one of Christ's first disciples. St. Joseph's discipleship began when Mary was betrothed to him and continued throughout the rest of his life as he led and loved within the Holy Family.

> "This is how Joseph of Nazareth was called, in turn, to become one of Jesus' disciples: by dedicating his life to serving the only-begotten Son of the Father and of his Virgin Mother, Mary. (Pope St. John Paul the Great, Homily March 19, 2001)

Look to St. Joseph to reveal to you the depth of humility required for true service of others.

Pause & Pray

Blessed St. Joseph,
Head of the Holy Family,
Increase your presence in my life.
By your intercession may I receive the grace to
Lead and love those entrusted to my care as you led
and Loved those entrusted to your care.
Amen.

Day 9

"And they did not understand the saying which he spoke to them. And he went down with them and came to Nazareth, and was obedient to them; and his mother kept all these things in her heart. And Jesus increased in wisdom and in stature, and in favor with God and man."

-Luke 2:50-52

This short line in the Gospel of Luke is all we have related to Christ's childhood. Luke jumps from the moment after Christ was found in the temple (age 12), right to the beginning of His public ministry (age 30) and uses this verse as the bridge. Any events that took place within those 18 years are hidden from us.

Goodness in the Hidden

One of the explanations for this "hidden life" is that God desired Christ to have a hidden, ordinary life in order to show the goodness of the ordinary life.

Jesus elevated the dignity of human nature by taking on human nature Himself. He showed us that having a human soul and a human body is good, by becoming man Himself (with a human body and human soul). If God is willing to take on a body Himself, it must mean that the human body is *good*.

This is why we can also say that the ordinary, hidden family life is good. God Incarnate did not enter human history in order to immediately begin preaching, teaching, and healing. Jesus entered the human story as an infant and spent the majority of His life simply being a part of a family. By living this way, Christ elevates the entire family experience, anoints it, and makes it holy.

Making a Holy Family

The elevation of family life does not mean that living out a holy family life is easy. We all know how absolutely messy family life can get. Whether we experienced it directly or indirectly, a poor family life can be one of the greatest sources of pain and often leads to deep emotional and spiritual wounds. But a good and holy family life can be the single greatest source of security and love in your life.

It is within the context of family that we are supposed to be introduced to unconditional love.

We should look to the example of Christ's hidden family life and try to make our own family life holy by safeguarding against all the ways our family life could be disrupted. Jesus spent years walking alongside Mary and St. Joseph. We should do the same.

Following Christ's example, we must allow Mary and St. Joseph to take on larger roles within our own family life. We must look to their examples of service to one another, and we must beg their intercession on our behalf. They who know intimately the struggles that face families are waiting to ask their Son to shower us with graces to become a holy family, too.

Perfecting the Ordinary

Grace perfects nature, and by the intercession of Mary and St. Joseph, grace can perfect the nature of the family. Pope St. John Paul the Great tells us that,

> "The family, which is founded and given life by love is a community of persons [...] without love the family is not a community of persons and, in the same way, without love the family cannot live, grow and perfect itself as a community of persons." (Familiaris Consortio, 18)

By its nature, the family is a community of persons founded and given in love. Every family is a community of love simply by the fact that it is a family. God wants to take this nature, and perfect it. It is through the family that He wants to form us authentically to love in communion. The love between members of the family,

> "is given life and sustenance by an unceasing inner dynamism leading the family to ever deeper and more intense communion, which is the foundation and soul of the community of marriage and the family." (Familiaris Consortio, 18)

It is within the ordinary family that Jesus experienced the intense communion of love. The communion of the Holy Family most closely resembles the communion between the persons of the Holy Trinity. The Holy Family is the result of grace perfecting family life.

Embracing the Ordinary

With Mary and St. Joseph, we can experience the living out of a grace-perfected family life. We do this by living, experiencing, and praying through the everyday realities of family life in our modern age. St. John Paul the Great tells that,

> "The Christian family also builds up the Kingdom of God in history through the everyday realities that concern and distinguish its state of life." (Familiaris Consortio, 50)

This means that we don't primarily build up the Kingdom by our time working and volunteering outside of the home or through a side hustle. We build up the Kingdom *within* the walls of family life. We should seek to live out our family life to the best of our ability and allow grace and love to perfect us where we are right now.

We must remember that God also moves outside of what most consider "religious." It is tempting to seek God only in the religious moments of our day, such as praying, Mass, and catechesis. But the Kingdom is also found within the mess and concerns of daily living. God can be found in ordinary human experience because He participated in it, within a family, and therefore He has anointed it.

When the Holy Family worked, ate, and played together, God was present, and saw that it was very good.

Go To Joseph

Go to Joseph so that he can intercede and protect your family life. If your family life is broken, he will intercede for healing. If your family life is difficult, he will intercede for an increase of grace. If your family life is uncertain, he will intercede for peace.

St. Joseph stood as protector of the Holy Family and wishes to be the protector of all families including yours. That is why he is waiting for us to ask of him for the Heavenly protection of a father.

Then by his example, embrace the ordinary moments of family life. Make the moments holy, by entering the ordinary wholly.

Go to Joseph and ask him to teach you how to live well in your family. God's waiting for your permission to allow grace to move, because it is within the family that lives can be transformed for Christ, and the world along with them.

Pause & Pray

Blessed St. Joseph,
Glory of home life,
Increase your presence in my life.
By your intercession may I receive the grace
to find God in the ordinary realities of family life.
Amen.

Day 10

"Is not this the carpenter's son? Is not his mother called Mary"

-Matthew 13:55

    St. Joseph lived a great life, but in the Gospel of Matthew we read that the crowds don't even remember his name. This speaks volumes of the deep contrast between what greatness looks like from the world's perspective and from God's.

    From the outsider's perspective, Joseph lived an ordinary life. To everyone who lived near and around the Holy Family, St. Joseph was a simple and ordinary poor man who worked hard to provide for his wife and child. But as we've uncovered in the last nine days, St. Joseph was anything but ordinary.

    Yet, the world didn't know what was Joseph's heart and that's why they refer to Jesus as the carpenter's son. Everything that we've come to learn of Joseph: his faith, obedience, courage, chastity, and countless other virtues, were exercised in hiddenness from the world. Every reason why he deserves all the titles given to him in litanies, went unnoticed by his peers. He was just a carpenter.

Hard At Work

In his hidden exercise of virtue we gain another glimpse into how St. Joseph lived as Jesus would later teach. Joseph embodied Christ's teachings of how to serve others. When Joseph served, he was more concerned with the service of God than the recognition from man. In the Sermon on the Mount Jesus tells us,

> "Take care not to perform righteous deeds in order that people may see them; otherwise, you will have no recompense from your heavenly Father." (Mt 6:1)

This is how St. Joseph lived. No one knew of his righteousness. All that he did was held within the Holy Family because it was them that he served, no one else.

We can also contemplate God's choice of an earthly father for Jesus. We learn more of the heart of God from what He found necessary for the foster-father of His Son. God did not choose a king or a rich man, with many servants. Instead, He chose a poor man who needed to work to provide. God did not find embarrassment in the need to work, and this brings tremendous dignity to the working family.

God not only chose Christ's father to be a working man, but He chose to work alongside him. St. Joseph would have brought Jesus to work with him and Joseph would have mentored Jesus as He learned His father's trade.

God shows us what He values by what He did with His time on earth. God was on earth for 33 years and made sure to spend a good portion of that time working with His dad.

Not only did Jesus redeem our human nature and family life, but He also redeemed ordinary human work. This redemption is exemplified in His work with St. Joseph. St. John Paul points out that,

> "Human work, and especially manual labor, receive special prominence in the Gospel. Along with the humanity of the Son of God, work too has been taken up in the mystery of the Incarnation, and has also been redeemed in a special way. At the workbench where he plied his trade together with Jesus, Joseph brought human work closer to the mystery of the Redemption. (Redemptoris Custos, 22)

Hidden Work

A life modeled after St. Joseph puts in the work spiritually and physically. The physical work, our daily jobs and responsibilities, should be done to the best of our ability in order to glorify God and serve others. But we shouldn't stop at the physical work, we must do the interior, spiritual work as well.

The spiritual work is our continued pursuit of holiness. That work continued as you began the preparation for Consecration, and it must continue afterwards.

As we come to the end of our preparation, we must resolve to do the work following St. Joseph's example and remember that the glory that comes with this work will not be seen by the world.

The world will not glorify your virtue and may end up remembering you as "just a carpenter." But the work will make an eternity of difference for you and those closest to you. Your family, close friends, and all whom you serve will experience the fruit of your hidden work.

Go To Joseph

Go to Joseph today and let him show you the value of hidden virtue and good work. In a culture where we are taught to equate success with recognition, wealth, and lack of responsibility, St. Joseph stands as a contradiction. He is a righteous carpenter elevated to the office of Patron of the Universal Church!

The changes that occur in your life after this consecration may not be seen by anyone outside of those closest to you. Like St. Joseph, you will be given a chance to live out hidden virtues and given an opportunity to continue doing ordinary work.

Go to Joseph and ask him to teach you how to find Jesus in the tabernacle and in the workbench.

Pause & Pray

Blessed St. Joseph,
Lover of poverty,
Increase your presence in my life.
By your intercession may I receive the grace to
Let my virtue and my work be for God's glory and
not my own.
Amen.

Consecration Day

New Beginning

You did it! You've spent the last 10 days contemplating the life of St. Joseph and uncovered the depth of his impact in his relationship to Jesus and Mary.

There are so many things that could be written and contemplated regarding St. Joseph, and this consecration is just a start. Don't think of this day as an end, but as a beginning. This is the beginning of your new relationship with this great Saint, and it is the beginning of a new path to Jesus, through St. Joseph.

Before you jump into the Act of Consecration, here are a few ways you can make sure this day is as impactful as it should be. Though your relationship with St. Joseph and Jesus should continue to mature beyond today, it is important to make time for God to enter this day. This is not a day that should be rushed through and the consecration should not be done in a hurry. Make time and pause from the craziness of life and allow God to do something new in your heart.

Celebrate

Celebrate this day, by making your consecration liturgical. You don't *have* to go to Holy Mass today, you *get* to go to Holy Mass.

Our consecration should stretch our hearts and increase our desire to follow Jesus more closely. So today we go to the source and font of life in the Eucharist. The Sacraments will be the source of grace that continues the transformation that this consecration begins, so start with the Sacraments today.

Before you pray the Act of Consecration today, find a priest, go to confession, attend Mass, and, make your Act of Consecration to St. Joseph.

Before and After

This consecration marks a new stage in your spiritual life. In the same manner that a new baby changes and stretches the heart of a parent to love more than they could have previously imagined, this consecration will stretch your heart.

When you look back there will be your heart before consecration, and your heart after. From now on, you will be set apart for Jesus Christ, under the protection of St. Joseph!

Act of Consecration to Saint Joseph
(Inspired by the writings of Saint John Paul the Great)

Blessed Saint Joseph, into whose custody God entrusted His most precious treasures, I _____, entrust myself completely and entirely to your patronage and protection. Protect and provide for me as I strive to love Jesus, honor Mary, and serve my family by your holy and virtuous example.

Most perfect Protector, graciously assist me from Heaven in my struggle with the powers of darkness. Just as you defended the child Jesus from mortal danger, so too defend me from the snares of the enemy and from all adversity.

Most faithful Husband, give me your heart, that I may willingly put to death sinful desires for the sake of those whom you've entrusted under my care. In moments of temptation, protect me, dispel the lies of sin, and intercede for me, that the Lord may grant me your faithfulness.

Most excellent Father, give me your heart that may I serve those entrusted to my care as a participation in the saving mission of Christ. Aid me by your intercession as I strive to walk before God in the ways of holiness and justice, seeking to faithfully carry out God's commands.

Most humble Worker, give me a heart that longs to serve God above all things. May my daily work bring the greatest glory to God.

Blessed Saint Joseph, Guardian of the Redeemer, give me your heart, and obtain for me this day the blessing of the Father, Son and Holy Spirit. Amen.

After Your Consecration

The Work Continues

Though we should expect a change, we shouldn't be troubled if we still encounter hardships, struggles and suffering. Jesus did not promise to deliver us from all suffering in this life, but He did promise that He would be with us until the end of time.

Your consecration to St. Joseph is a reminder of Christ's promise. Christ will be with you daily *through* St. Joseph. You are adopted by a spiritual father who will not abandon you and who will work tirelessly to bring you close to his Son.

Whatever the future might bring, you are not alone. You have St. Joseph's example of how to live and love Christ. Take comfort in knowing that He is a good God, and He is with you always.

Renewing Your Consecration

You should renew your consecration annually. This helps you return to devotion if you have fallen away from it, and it helps strengthen your consecration as you remind yourself why you choose this path in the first place.

You don't have to use this book the next time around! There is a list of other popular St. Joseph titles at the end of this book.

Share this Consecration

My whole purpose for writing this book was to increase devotion to St. Joseph. Consecration to Jesus through St. Joseph has brought me closer to Christ than I could have ever imagined, and I wanted to share that with others.

Now it's your turn. Share this devotion with other people. Let them know how God is working in your life through St. Joseph and share this, or other consecration books with them so they can consecrate themselves as well. In this way we will continue to bring hearts to Jesus through the powerful intercession of St. Joseph.

Increase Your Devotion

From this day forward, you are under the powerful patronage and protection of St. Joseph. Don't let him become a stranger again. It is easy to be excited about this new devotion for a few days or weeks and then fall back into our old habits. That is why we should make a point to seek out St. Joseph and his powerful intercession every day.

By adding at least one St. Joseph prayer to your prayer life, you can remind yourself of your consecration and you can continue the work that God is doing through St. Joseph in you. To help, I have included some of the most popular St. Joseph prayers, as well as a short entrustment prayer that can be said daily.

Go To Joseph
Daily Prayer of Entrustment

Blessed St. Joseph, I entrust myself totally to your patronage and protection. Guard me as I strive to love Jesus and honor Mary by your holy and virtuous example. Let my life bring the greatest glory to God this day. Amen

Prayers to St. Joseph

Novena Prayer to St. Joseph
(To be said consecutively for nine days)

Oh, St. Joseph, whose protection is so great, so prompt, so strong, before the throne of God, I place in you all my interests and desires.

Oh, St. Joseph, do assist me by your powerful intercession, and obtain for me from your Divine Son
all spiritual blessings, through Jesus Christ, our Lord.
So that, having engaged here below your heavenly power, I may offer my thanksgiving and homage to the most loving of fathers.

Oh, St. Joseph, I never weary contemplating you and Jesus asleep in your arms; I dare not approach while He reposes near your heart. Press Him in my name and kiss His fine head for me and ask Him to return the kiss when I draw my dying breath.

St. Joseph, patron of departing souls, pray for me. Amen.

Memorare to St. Joseph

Remember, O most chaste spouse of the Virgin Mary, that never was it known that anyone who implored your help and sought your intercession were left unassisted. Full of confidence in your power I fly unto you and beg your protection. Despise not O Guardian of the Redeemer my humble supplication, but in your bounty, hear and answer me. Amen.

Litany of St. Joseph

Lord, have mercy on us.
Christ, have mercy on us.
Lord, have mercy on us. Christ, hear us.
Christ, graciously hear us.

God the Father of Heaven, *have mercy on us.*
God the Son, Redeemer of the world, *have mercy on us.*
God the Holy Ghost, *have mercy on us.*
Holy Trinity, One God, *have mercy on us.*

Holy Mary, *pray for us.*
St. Joseph, *pray for us.*
Illustrious son of David, *pray for us.*
Light of patriarchs, *pray for us.*
Spouse of the Mother of God, *pray for us.*
Chaste guardian of the Virgin, *pray for us.*
Foster father of the Son of God, *pray for us.*
Watchful defender of Christ, *pray for us.*
Head of the Holy Family, *pray for us.*

Joseph most just, *pray for us.*
Joseph most chaste, *pray for us.*
Joseph most prudent, *pray for us.*
Joseph most valiant, *pray for us.*
Joseph most obedient, *pray for us.*
Joseph most faithful, *pray for us.*
Mirror of patience, *pray for us.*
Lover of poverty, *pray for us.*
Model of workmen, *pray for us.*
Glory of home life, *pray for us.*
Guardian of virgins, *pray for us.*
Pillar of families, *pray for us.*
Solace of the afflicted, *pray for us.*
Hope of the sick, *pray for us.*

Patron of the dying, *pray for us.*
Terror of demons, *pray for us.*
Protector of the Holy Church, *pray for us.*

Lamb of God, Who takes away the sins of the world,
Spare us, O Lord!
Lamb of God, Who takes away the sins of the world,
Graciously hear us, O Lord!
Lamb of God, Who takes away the sins of the world,
Have mercy on us!

V. He made him the lord of His household,
R. *And prince over all His possessions.*
Let Us Pray

O God, Who in Thine ineffable Providence didst vouchsafe to choose Blessed Joseph to be the spouse of Thy most holy Mother, grant, we beseech Thee, that he whom we venerate as our protector on earth may be our intercessor in Heaven. Who lives and reigns forever and ever. Amen.

Prayer Before Work

O Glorious Saint Joseph, model of all those who are devoted to labor, obtain for me the grace to work in a spirit of penance for the expiation of my many sins; to work conscientiously, putting the call of duty above my natural inclinations; to work with thankfulness and joy, considering it an honor to employ and develop by means of labor the gifts received from God; to work with order, peace, moderation, and patience, never shrinking from weariness and trials; to work above all with purity of intention and detachment from self,
keeping unceasingly before my eyes death and the account that I must give of time lost, talents unused, good omitted, and vain complacency in success, so fatal to the work of God.

All for Jesus, all through Mary, all after thy example, O Patriarch, Saint Joseph. Such shall be my watchword in life and in death. Amen.

(Composed by Pope St. Pius X)

Prayer for the Year of St. Joseph

Hail, Guardian of the Redeemer,
Spouse of the Blessed Virgin Mary.
To you God entrusted his only Son;
in you Mary placed her trust;
with you Christ became man.

Blessed Joseph, to us too,
show yourself a father
and guide us in the path of life.
Obtain for us grace, mercy and courage,
and defend us from every evil. Amen.

- Pope Francis (Patris Corde, December 8, 2020)

Prayer to St. Joseph After the Rosary

This prayer to Saint Joseph was composed by Pope Leo XIII in his 1889 encyclical, Quamquam Pluries. He asked that it be added to the end of the Rosary, especially during the month of October, which is dedicated to the Rosary.

To you, O blessed Joseph,
do we come in our tribulation,
and having implored the help of your most holy Spouse, we confidently invoke your patronage also.

Through that charity which bound you
to the Immaculate Virgin Mother of God
and through the paternal love
with which you embraced the Child Jesus,
we humbly beg you graciously to regard the inheritance
which Jesus Christ has purchased by his Blood,
and with your power and strength to aid us in our necessities.
O most watchful guardian of the Holy Family,
defend the chosen children of Jesus Christ;
O most loving father, ward off from us
every contagion of error and corrupting influence;
O our most mighty protector, be kind to us
and from heaven assist us in our struggle
with the power of darkness.

As once you rescued the Child Jesus from deadly peril, so now protect God's Holy Church
from the snares of the enemy and from all adversity; shield, too, each one of us by your constant protection,
so that, supported by your example and your aid,
we may be able to live piously, to die in holiness,
and to obtain eternal happiness in heaven. Amen.

Prayer For a Happy death

O Blessed Joseph, you gave your last breath in the loving embrace of Jesus and Mary. When the seal of death shall close my life, come with Jesus and Mary to aid me. Obtain for me this solace for that hour - to die with their holy arms around me. Jesus, Mary and Joseph, I commend my soul, living and dying, into your sacred arms. Amen.

About the Author

Renzo Ortega is a graduate Theology student at Holy Apostles College & Seminary. He and his wife are founders of Two Become Family, a marriage and family accompaniment ministry. Together, they aim to bring the Gospel to families and empower them to become what they are. The Ortegas live in Connecticut with their five children and serve in youth ministry and marriage ministry at their home parish.

Two Become Family

At Two Become Family, our goal is to restore confidence in family life again. St. John Paul accurately portrays the state of many families today when he said, "The modern Christian family is often tempted to be discouraged and is distressed at the growth of its difficulties."

There are so many difficulties that families face. You would be hard-pressed to find a family, including us, that would claim that they did *not* experience any difficulties while navigating family life.

We are not here to tell families to follow *our* example or a five step process in order to find peace. Our goal is to encourage the family to have, "confidence in itself, in the riches that it possesses by nature and grace, and in the mission that God has entrusted to it."(Familiaris Consortio)

Every Catholic family possesses all that it needs to succeed, by nature and by grace. In the midst of difficulties and hardships, families need not look beyond the Sacrament that binds them. Our articles, videos, Instagram posts, and any future content is directed towards that end. We want to give families confidence that they have what it takes.

You have what it takes to have an amazing marriage, to raise beautiful children, and to serve Christ and His Church *through* your family!

Learn More at TwoBecomeFamily.com

Leave a Review!

If you enjoyed this book, please consider leaving an honest review on Amazon!

Other Titles For Consecration to St. Joseph

Consecration to St. Joseph:
The Wonders of Our Spiritual Father
By Fr Donald Calloway

Consecration to Jesus through St. Joseph: An Integrated Look At the Holy Family

By Dr Greg Bottaro

Made in the USA
Coppell, TX
16 June 2021